What Did You Say?

A Book of Homophones

Words that sound the same but that look different and have different meanings.

by Sylvia Root Tester
illustrated by John Keely

THE CHILD'S WORLD

ELGIN, ILLINOIS 60120

Distributed by Childrens Press, 1224 West Van Buren Street, Chicago, Illinois 60607.

Library of Congress Cataloging in Publication Data

Tester, Sylvia Root, 1939-
  What did you say?

  (Using words)
  SUMMARY: Introduces homophones, words that sound the same but whose meaning and spelling is different.
    1. English language—Homonyms—Juvenile literature.
[1. English language—Homonyms] I. Title. II. Series.
PE1595.T43   423'.1   77-9494
ISBN 0-913778-91-5

dough

doe

pear

pair

pale

pail

wait

weight

beach

beech

creek

creak

heel

heal

My aunt makes very good cookies.

aunt

ant

throne

thrown

do – dew

knew — gnu

would –wood

ewe—you

peak

peek

hare

hair

close — clothes